Upside Down, Turn Me Around

BIBLE STORIES

Jesus Did What?

Written by Suzanne Slade
Illustrated by Dan Foote

Jesus did many miracles while he was on earth. Once, Jesus sent his disciples in a boat across the lake. Later, Jesus walked on top of the water to reach them.

Do you think Jesus walked on the water because he didn't want to get wet? Was he walking because he didn't know how to swim? No!

Jesus saw his friends were in trouble. A strong wind blew across the lake as the disciples tried to row to shore. They rowed and rowed with all their might, but the fierce wind and large waves kept them out at sea.

Jesus walked across the lake to the boat. At first the disciples were frightened when they saw Jesus. But he said, "It's me. Don't be afraid." After he climbed inside the boat, the wind died down and the disciples were amazed. Jesus walked on water to save his friends and show them he is God.

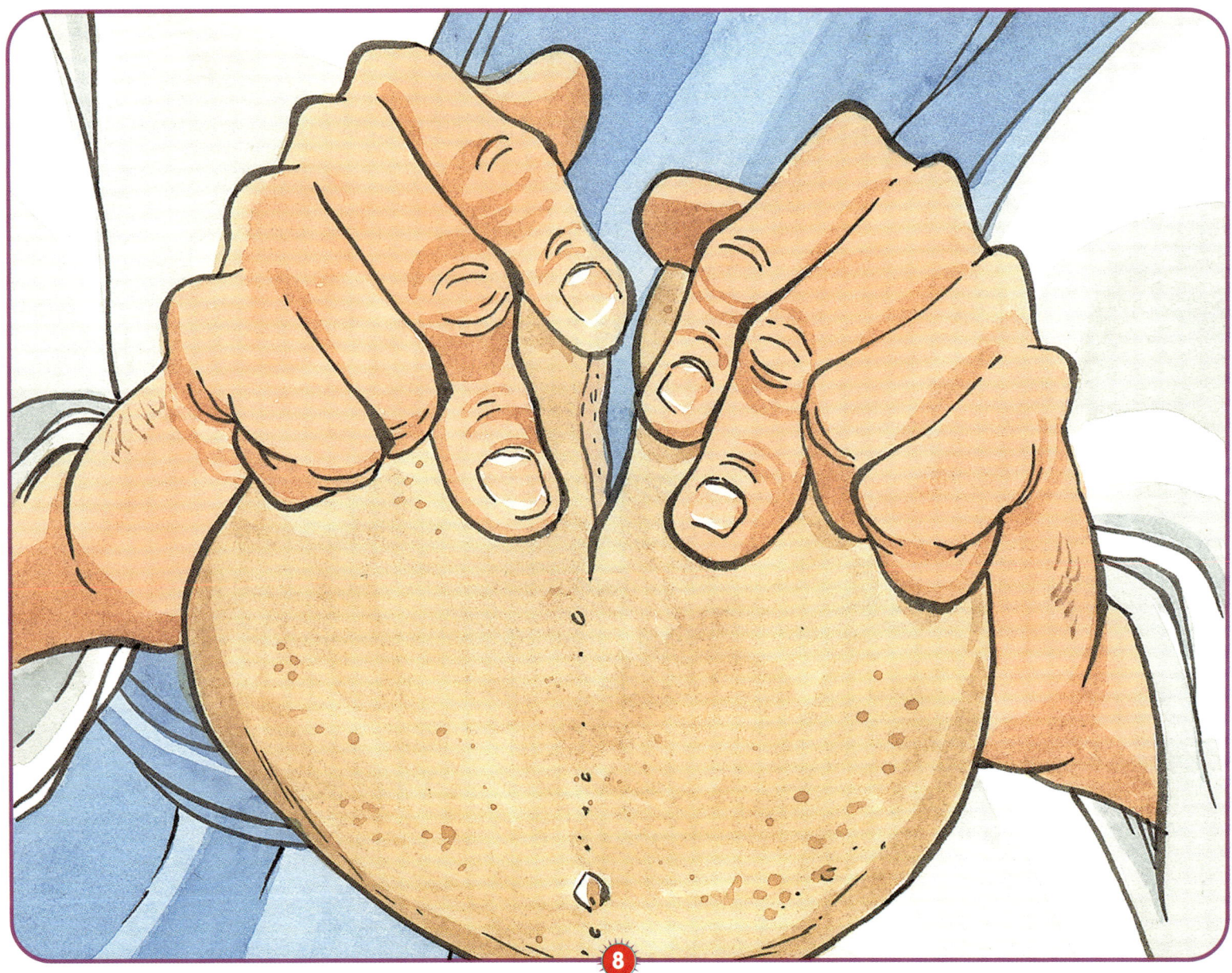

Another day, Jesus made a little food into a lot and fed a large crowd of people on a hill.

Do you think Jesus was so hungry that all he could think about was the rumbling in his stomach? Did Jesus break the bread so he could make himself a fish sandwich? No!

Jesus saw that the people were tired and hungry. He wanted to take care of the large crowd that had gathered to see him. A young boy offered his five pieces of bread and two fish to Jesus.

Jesus gave thanks for the food, broke the bread, and shared it with all the people. Five thousand people ate bread and fish that day until they were full. After everyone had finished eating, the disciples filled twelve baskets with leftovers. Jesus broke the bread to feed and care for his followers.

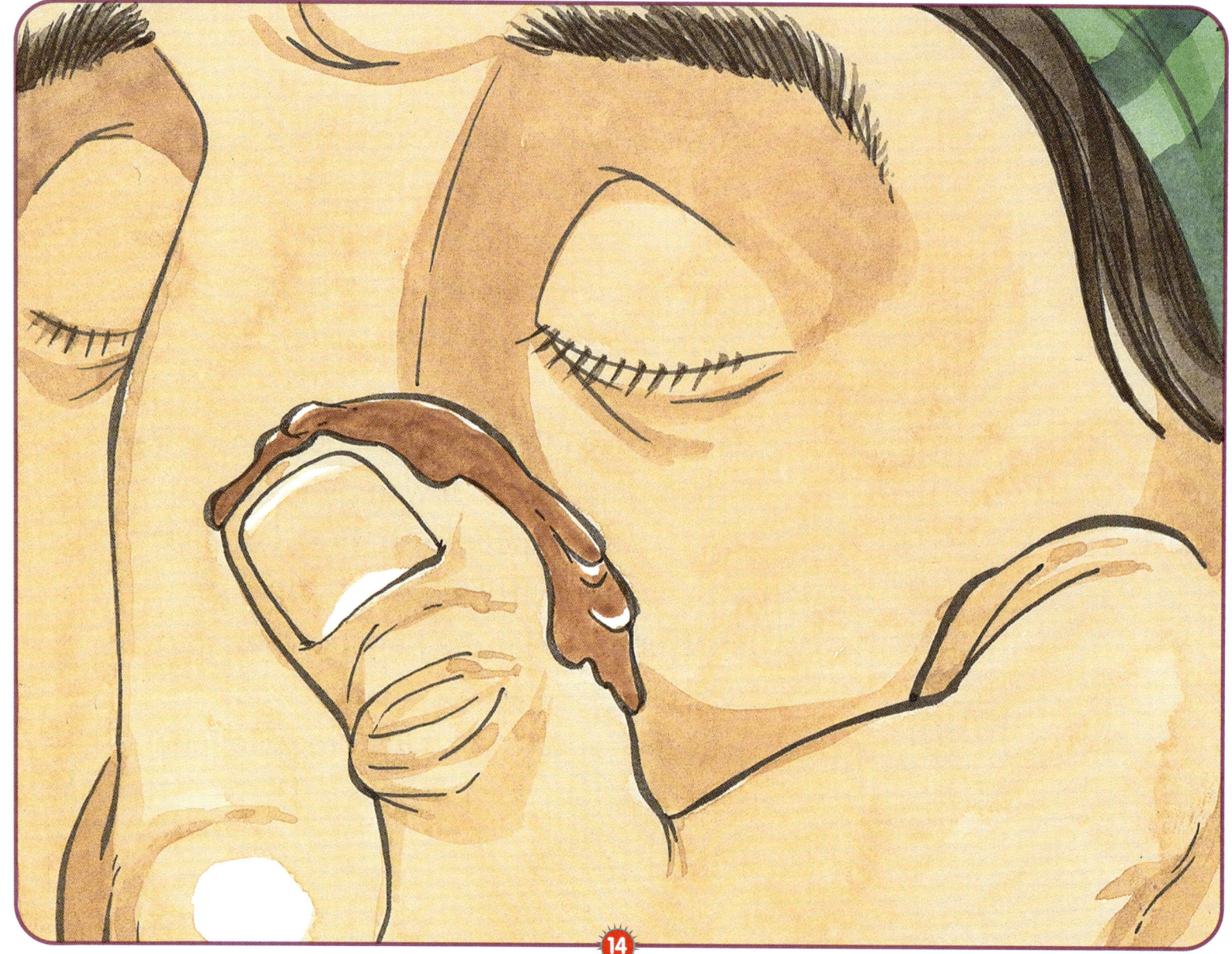

One day, Jesus mixed water and dirt to make mud. Then he put the mud on the eyes of a man who had been blind since he was born.

Do you think Jesus liked to play in the mud? Did he want to start a huge mud fight? Did he want to make the blind man look like a raccoon? Was he training for a mud-throwing contest? No!

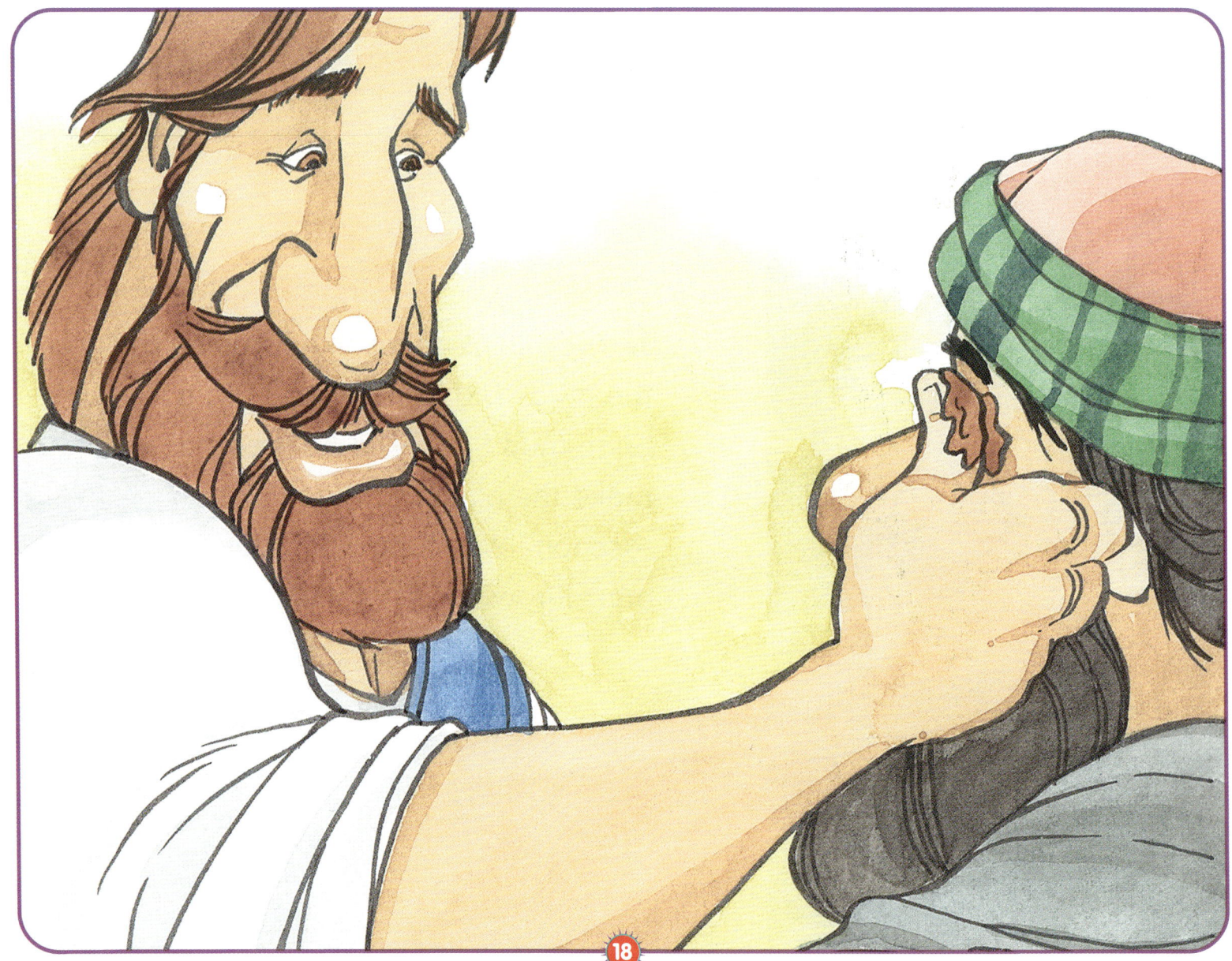

Jesus wanted to heal the blind man. He wanted others to see God's power. Jesus put mud on the man's eyes and then told him to go and wash the mud off in a pool.

After the blind man did what Jesus said, he was able to see. He could see green trees, blue sky, and all of God's beautiful creation. He even saw his parents for the very first time. He was so happy!

Jesus put mud on the blind man's eyes to give him sight and show everyone the mighty power of God. Jesus wants to open our eyes so we can see that he is our loving Savior.

Jesus Did What?

Life Issue: I want my child to trust in God.

Spiritual Building Block: Trust

Do the following activities to encourage your child to trust God:

Sight: Ask your child, *What do you think Jesus looks like?* Read the description of the Messiah in Isaiah 53:2. Then read the description of Jesus in Revelation 1:13–18. Invite your child to draw a picture, using crayons or markers, of what he or she thinks Jesus looks like.

Sound: Read Jesus' first four words in Revelation 1:17 to your child: "Do not be afraid." Talk about what your child can do when he or she is afraid. For example: pray to Jesus, sing a church song, recite a Bible verse.

Touch: Act out the story of Jesus walking on the water and calming the storm. Using a laundry basket or rocking chair for the boat, you and your child can pretend to be scared until you see Jesus and hear him say, "It is I; don't be afraid." Then pretend to be on a calm sea. Remind your child that we can always tell Jesus about our fears. Then we'll remember that he's with us and cares when we feel afraid.

Upside Down, Turn Me Around

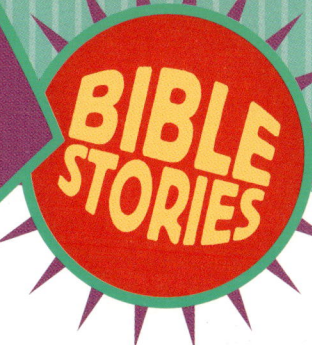

BIBLE STORIES

Jesus Said What?

Written by Suzanne Slade
Illustrated by Terry Julien

Faith Kidz® is an imprint of
Cook Communications Ministries, Colorado Springs, CO 80918
Cook Communications, Paris, Ontario
Kingsway Communications, Eastbourne, England

JESUS SAID WHAT?
© 2006 by Cook Communications Ministries for text and illustrations

All rights reserved. No part of this book may be reproduced without written permission, except for brief quotations in books and critical reviews. For information, write Cook Communications Ministries, 4050 Lee Vance View, Colorado Springs, CO 80918.

First Printing, 2006
Printed in India
1 2 3 4 5 6 7 8 9 10 Printing/Year 10 09 08 07 06

Cover and Interior Design: Sandy Flewelling

Unless otherwise noted, Scripture quotations are taken from the HOLY BIBLE: NEW INTERNATIONAL VERSION®. Copyright © 1973, 1978, 1984 by International Bible Society. Used by permission of Zondervan Publishing House. All rights reserved.

ISBN: 0781443482

Jesus Said What?

Jesus said, "I am the good shepherd; I know my sheep and my sheep know me."

Do you think Jesus came to earth so he could be a shepherd and play with sheep? Did Jesus like to count sheep? No!

Jesus didn't come to sit around with sheep all day and knit wool sweaters.

Jesus said, "I am the good shepherd; I know my sheep and my sheep know me" because he loves you. He cares for you just like a shepherd watches over his sheep.

Jesus knows and loves every one of his children. He takes good care of his flock of followers and watches over you day and night.

Jesus said, "The very hairs on your head are counted."

Do you think Jesus spent his time counting the hairs on people's heads? Did people travel from miles around to line up and have their hairs counted? No!

Jesus didn't count the hairs on anyone's head. He said, "The very hairs on your head are counted" to show you how important you are to him. He is interested in the big things in your life, as well as the small, tiny details. Jesus loves you very much!

Jesus said, "You must be born again."

Do you think Jesus said that because he wanted more birthday parties? Did he just want to celebrate birthdays and eat cake all the time? No!

You don't have two birthdays when you are born again.

Jesus said, "You must be born again" to tell how you can belong to God's family. Jesus wants everyone to belong to God's family. He doesn't want anyone to be left out.

When you ask Jesus to be in charge of your life and trust him to forgive your sins, then you are born again. It feels great to belong to Jesus because he always loves you and knows what is best for you.

Jesus Said What?

Life Issue: I want my child to know that God is faithful to us.

Spiritual Building Block: Faithfulness

Help your child learn about God's faithfulness in the following ways:

Sight: Have your child look at one of the pictures in this story for twenty seconds. Close the book and ask your child to list as many items as he or she can remember in the picture. Let your child look at the picture again to see what items were missed. Now look at a different picture and see how many items you can remember. Tell your child that God always remembers us.

Sound: Say two words to describe God. For example: *God is kind and faithful.* Ask your child to repeat the sentence and add a word. *God is kind, faithful, and big!* Then you say the sentence and add another word. Do this until someone forgets a word or says them out of order. (Your child may have to play this game several times to build up to remembering seven words that describe God.)

Touch: Help your child understand what a shepherd does for his sheep by acting it out together. As a shepherd, you can lead your lamb (your child) to water, protect her from a wild (stuffed) animal, and watch over her while she pretends to eat or sleep. Then talk together about how Jesus cares for us in similar ways.

Upside Down, Turn Me Around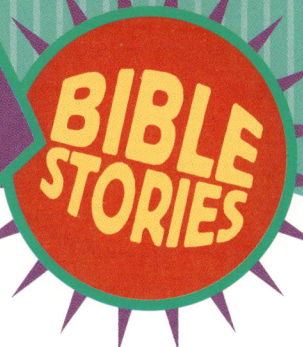

BIBLE STORIES

Jesus Says

**Written by Heather Gemmen
and Mary McNeil**

Illustrated by Dan Foote

"Sometimes people say, 'Hate your enemy.'

I say, 'Love your enemies.'"

What should we do?

"Sometimes people say, 'Don't break a promise.'

I say, 'Don't make promises you can't keep.'"

What should we do?

"Sometimes people say, 'Hurt the person who hurt you.'

I say, 'Love the people who hurt you.'"

What should we do?

Let's do what Jesus says!

Jesus Says

Life Issue: I want my child to follow Jesus' example.

Spiritual Building Block: Discipleship

Do the following activities to help your child to follow Jesus' example:

Sight: As you read stories or watch movies together, talk about different situations you see. Ask your child *"What would Jesus do?"* in each situation and encourage your child to follow Jesus' example.

Sound: One way to love our enemies is to pray for them. Teach your child to pray for others, not just family and friends.

Touch: Talk with your child about different ways to be kind to people who have not treated him nicely. Then practice those ways with a doll or stuffed animal.